Metamorphosis

THE TRANSFORMATION OF A SOUL

Frank Duprée

ACKNOWLEDGMENTS

I'd like to acknowledge several people who have been a vital part of the transformation of my soul. The late Dr. Wade E. Taylor author and found of Pinecrest Bible Training Center, NY. "Brother Taylor", as he was known, always focused on the interior life of prayer and meditation in The Word of God.

Also, my wife, Giovanna. She has helped me to stay in "the great struggle". Her spiritual strength and determination to see God's will in her life has been an inspiration to me personally as well as to many others.

DEDICATION

This short story is dedicated to all those who are in "the process" of transformation. In the King James Version of the Holy Bible we find that Jesus was "transfigured" on the Mount. Paul the Apostle talks about our personal "transformation" in several places.

In the original language that the Bible was written in we find that both of these words come from the Greek word for "Metamorphosis". Thus, the title of this book.

Press on… change is taking place. Have courage and you will see the end result and be glad!

Metamorphosis

Frank Duprée

CONTENTS

Acknowledgments i
ii
Dedication

The Cocoon 1

Bookends Pg 9

Choices Pg 16

Application Pg 19

He Made Up His Mind Pg 22

Did You Hear About Pat? Pg 24

THE COCOON

It was noontime. My workload was unbelievable. Calls to return, reports to read and reports to write. How would I ever get through it all? I was dazed. I should have walked out, taken my lunch break, and come right back to the office, but I didn't. I picked up my jacket and walked, or should I say I drifted, out the door. I wandered down the street past the vendors and the lunchtime crowds. I was walking in the park. What streets did I take? I don't know. But there I was, a lost soul, wandering around. I can't remember ever feeling so numb to the world.

I will never forget that day. It is etched into my memory. How did I ever become what I was then? I was unfulfilled, overweight, and tired of the rat race. I was married to the girl of my dreams and had two children whom I loved to pieces. But lately even my home life was not what it should have been. We weren't talking much; I was even out of touch with my kids. For a while I had buried myself in sports, but it didn't take long before the thrill was gone, and I just stopped playing. I had always thought that if I worked hard and did the best I could I would succeed in life. It seemed that success was eluding me. I just seemed to be on a treadmill, going nowhere. The bills were piling up higher and higher. My ambition and drive were getting lower and lower.

As I was walking along, a line from an old song kept playing in my head: "been dazed and confused for so long it's not true." That's how I felt, dazed and confused. The next thing I knew I was in the park. I know there were children all about, but I wasn't paying any attention to their games and noise they made. There were people reading books, some folks playing checkers, and a dog fetching a stick. They looked like they were having such a good time, but it just made me feel worse.

I wandered over to the lake and walked beside the water. That's when I saw it. What was it? Something was hanging on a branch, just over the water edge. It was a chrysalis. I don't know how long I stood there looking at it but it didn't matter. For some reason it made me feel good. I think I was identifying with it. I felt like I was shut up in some kind of cocoon. I was suffocating inside. I felt like I was dying.

That's when something happened that I never expected. I had never seen it happen before. I saw the cocoon start to move. Whatever was inside was trying to get out. Boy, did I identify with that! I had to get out of my cocoon too. My sense of dying started to change. A feeling of excitement started to fill me up all over. It was electrifying. My sense of suffocation was replaced with an increased zest for life. Every time that butterfly pushed against that cocoon I pushed against mine. Time was standing still. Was it an hour or the whole afternoon? I don't know. But I do know what happened next.

That butterfly was struggling so hard all by itself. Just like me. I decided to help it out. I got out my pocket knife, opened it and carefully cut a tiny slit the cocoon. In just a few minutes the butterfly was making its way out. I felt great! That's what I needed. Someone to help me. I needed a break. I was working so hard trying to be the best that I could be, but it wasn't working. I guess that's why I felt so close to that butterfly. I even imagined that its smiled at me as it worked itself out of the cocoon. As I looked at it glistening in the sunlight, I felt good.
There it was hanging upside down and flapping its wings. I wondered how long it would be before it flew away, soaring up into the sky. Those few minutes watching that butterfly were some of the most exciting minutes I had ever spent. But it didn't fly away. It stopped flapping its wings. After a moment or two it started to flap to them again. But it didn't flap them as hard this time. It soon stopped, and then after a moment it started flapping them again; but this time it was for an even shorter time. Then it just hung there, and then it dropped into the lake and drowned.

It just floated away, and as it did all my emotions floated away too. I felt like I died along with that butterfly. What happened? Although the sun was shining brightly a dark cloud seemed to cover my head. Was that what was going to happen to me? Was I going to hang on just a little while longer and then drop and die? I walked away feeling sad. I had felt bad when I walked into the park, and now I felt totally depressed. I just wandered around.

Something happened as I was walking. I seemed to go back to elementary school and I was just a boy again. There I was in science class and my teacher was holding a stick with a chrysalis on it. It was as clear in my mind as if I was there again. She started to tell us about the change that a caterpillar goes through in its chrysalis. I can see her standing there right now and I hear her voice again. "When the time comes for the caterpillar to change into a butterfly it spins a cocoon around itself. Once the cocoon is finished the change starts to take place. Everything about the caterpillar becomes different. What will emerge later on after a great struggle is not a caterpillar with wings but a new creature! It is a butterfly!"

I saw it. I heard it. I remembered everything. Why didn't it work? I replayed it in my mind over again. I must have forgotten something. Then it struck me. "After a great struggle." That was it! I thought that butterfly needed help, but it didn't. It had everything it needed. God had given it everything it needed already. To make that change from caterpillar to butterfly was easy. It wasn't hard to spin the cocoon. And once inside the change took place all by itself. The hard part was getting out of the cocoon. That was where the struggle was. No! That was where the "great struggle" was! That butterfly didn't really need a break. I didn't help it at all. I had killed it!

Boy did I feel bad! But the depression didn't stay... It seemed to float away. Something was happening inside of me. Somehow I didn't feel that the butterfly's life was wasted. I felt as if it had fulfilled its destiny. I know now that that butterfly taught me the most important lesson I had ever learned in my entire life. God had put in me everything I needed for my life to change. That was the day I decided that I was going to go through my own "great struggle" and break out of the cocoon I had formed around myself.

I started walking out of the park. I remember thinking to myself that I didn't need a break after all. I made up my mind that I wasn't going to stay in my cocoon any longer. I was going to make that butterfly the symbol of my life. When I tried to help that butterfly out of its cocoon, I took away from it the one thing it needed to be able to fly. It needed that "great struggle" in order to build the strength to fly.

Whatever struggles I would face from that day on, I would face them knowing that God had put inside of me the ability to go through whatever was necessary. I was going to work through my problems. Every single one of them! I was going to get my career back on track. In fact, I was going to make the changes necessary to go forward and achieve some of those things that I had put off because I thought they were unattainable. I was going to work through my family problems.

I decided right there and then that I was going to start to communicate with my wife and children and have that happy family I always wanted. And last of all I was going to go through whatever struggles I faced in order to change myself. I felt that something was happening deep in my soul. Somehow there was a kind of metamorphosis going on.

The mere fact that I realized my struggles were necessary seemed to get the process going. I wasn't going to go through life looking for a break anymore. I wasn't going to be like a caterpillar going through life with my head hanging down every day. I was going to be metamorphosised: transformed into a butterfly and soar through life. I was going to fulfill my destiny.

That was the day I stopped feeling sorry for myself and hoping someone would give me a break. I found out what my soul knew all long. I realized that God has placed in us, every one of us, the ability and then the opportunity to have a metamorphosis. Mine had begun.

BOOKENDS

When they say "Time flies," they really mean it! It had been months since I saw the chrysalis and started my metamorphosis, and yet it felt as if only a few days had passed. I was happy that day. I had the day off! Just me! Barb was going to work, and the kids had already left for school. I had the whole day to myself and could do whatever I wanted without feeling guilty about it! I didn't feel like playing golf or tennis, and I didn't want to run either. Boy, the biggest problem I had that day was deciding how to goof off!

Barb and I had really been doing well. After I had told her about the chrysalis and what had happened to me it seemed as if we had gotten off to a new start in our relationship. We spent hours talking just like we did when we first met. I was able to rekindle that romantic spark inside of me; and no matter what was going on around us, we would look at each other, and that "knowing" was there again just like before. We knew everything would work out. It was like someone said in the Bible; "God will make a way where there is no way."

That's another thing that was really great; my spiritual life. I never really had one before. I kind of believed in God, but I didn't know anything about religion or faith. Now I believed that He had some sort of plan or something and that everything was working according to it. I didn't feel "spooky" or anything. I just had a kind of trust or something, and things that I'd heard people say about the Bible came to my mind, and I kind of knew they were true.

Well, anyway, I got dressed and decided to take a walk downtown to the "hippie" neighborhood. At least that's what some people called it. It was the area where there were some great coffee shops and bookstores and I just felt like finding a great book and curling up in a chair and reading for a while. What was really great about the kind of places down there was that you didn't even have to buy the book if you didn't want to. Just read a bit of it and see if you like it. If you did, you bought it. If not, you shelved it. "Kind of like taking a car out for a test drive," Barb said. I don't know who came up with the idea, but I liked it.

What a day it was too. One of those days where the oranges and greens of the plants and leaves kind of melted together as you walked along. I loved the fall. I really did. I almost just kept walking but as I passed the entrance to the bookstore I "knew" it was the place to stroll into. There it was again. That "knowing". Weird, but kinda comfortable too. I just went with the flow.

I thought I saw a butterfly as I walked in, but it couldn't have been one. It was too late in the year, but I think I was being set up. Know what I mean? Well, I browsed around with a cappuccino in my hand. It was good. The smell of espresso makes my senses come alive. The girl making the cappuccino knew her stuff, too. She didn't scald the milk like so many people did. There's nothing worse than a cappuccino that is too hot with scalded milk. I had a book or two in the other hand. Nothing great, but they'd work for a while.

Just as I was looking for a place to sit down I saw these great bookends on one of the shelves. I'd never seen any bookends like those before, and I liked them so much I figured I'd ask if they were for sale. They were unique, really different. The left one was a Madonna and Baby and the right one was a copy of the "Pieta" by Michelangelo. And to top it off, the book against the left one was called simply "BIRTH," and the book against the right one was called "DEATH." They fit because the left one was the Madonna holding the baby Jesus at his birth and the right one was the Madonna holding the crucified body of Jesus in his death.

As I was looking at them a man came up next to me and asked me what I thought of his bookends. I told him how much I liked them and that I wanted to purchase them. He was the shopkeeper, a nice looking guy. Not a "hippie" type at all. Well, maybe he had been a hippie earlier in life, but he wasn't now. He was dressed in a casual sort of way. No beard and I thought all bookstore owners had beards. No, he seemed to be your average guy.

Nothing in him that would make him stand out in a crowd. But he did have a great smile and a great laugh too! When I told him about the "birth and death" books and how they fit the bookends he laughed a big, hearty laugh. One like I used to laugh when I was a kid when something struck me real funny. That laugh struck a chord in me, and I felt like I knew this guy when I had only just met him.

"That's what they're supposed to evoke in you. But do you know what? Hardly anyone ever mentions it. They look at them. They see the books and then they walk away."

I wondered why, but then he asked me: "What do you see in them?"

I told him that they brought back to my mind something that happened to me a few months ago, something that really affected me. He moved over to a couple of easy chairs and told me to sit down.

"I'd love to hear about it," he said.

Well, an hour or two and a cappuccino or two later. I wrapped it up by telling him how I was undergoing my own metamorphosis, then he said the strangest thing to me.

"I've been waiting for you to come here."

I was taken back and the "Twilight Zone" music started playing in my head. I heard myself ask him:

"What do you mean, you've been waiting for me?

He started to get up and said, "You probably have to be going, don't you"?

Now I was really shocked! Here's this guy I just meet, somehow he gets me to open up my life and spill my guts to him and then says he's been waiting for me, but you probably have to go, don't you? I sat right where I was and said: "No, I don't have to go anywhere.

What do you mean?"

He sat back down, "I'm glad you said that. I really like you".

What did he mean, well I knew what he meant. But it took me by surprise. I really liked him too. We had kinda clicked. You know?

He said that he was sorry he had sort of "bummed me out" by what he said, but that he was just checking to see if I was ready for the next level. "Next level of what?" I asked him.

"The next level of your metamorphosis," he said.

Now, there was something really strange about this conversation, but I knew; there it was again, that it was OK. How I knew that, I don't know, but I knew it. He started talking about the bookends again. "Birth and Death, two things you have no choice in, right?"

"Yeah, that's right. You don't ask to be born, but here you are; and whether you want to or not, you're going to die. So you're right, those are two things you've got no choice in."

"Well," he said, "those are the bookends of our lives. Just like books are arranged on a shelf, our lives are arranged by God on His shelf."

That sounded spiritual, but good. I liked it right away. Yeah, God placed the bookends of my life on one of his shelves, and now He was writing the story. The owner must have known what I was thinking because he said,

"No, you're wrong."

Boy, what was he, a mind reader? I heard that some of the "new age" people believed in that stuff, but I didn't know anyone who did it. Then he did it again;

"No, I'm not reading your mind. I just know where you're at; so, I know you're wrong."

"So, what am I wrong about?" I asked.

"About God writing the story of your life."

Somehow I knew he really did know where I was at. How could he have known that's what I was thinking, if he didn't?

"What do you mean?"

"Well, you understand about the 'birth and death' aspect but it's not God writing the story. He's just giving you the inspiration to be the best you can be. Let's go look at the bookends again."

We went over there and looked at them. They were beautiful. They we very provocative.

"What's in between them?" he asked.

" 'Call of the Wild,' 'Cry of the Wolf,' 'Chance and Luck.' Nothing but books that begin with the letter C."

"That's right. There's nothing but Cs in between B and D. Do you know why?"

Well, I knew right away that it was a two-part question. You know what I mean? One part is the obvious, because that's the way the alphabet is. But the not so obvious - that's what he was asking about. I knew that too. I told him as much.

"Well, yes, that's the way the alphabet is, and yes, there is a deeper answer. First the natural then the spiritual.

"What do you mean?" I asked.

"The Bible teaches us that God always shows us important spiritual truths through nature first, then in the spiritual world. That's why so many people love to read the Bible. They love to find the spiritual truths that are buried in it like diamonds in a mine."

I couldn't help but think that that idea made a lot of sense, and it made me want to know the spiritual truth that he was going to share with me even more.

"So what's the spiritual truth in the bookends? Why are there only C's in between 'Birth and Death'?"

"I'm glad you put it that way," he said. "Most people would not have phrased it that way. It shows you're well on the way into your spiritual journey, or metamorphosis as you call it. "The C's are for all the choices you will make during your journey from birth to death. You have no choice in the beginning nor at the end, but in between, it's all up to you! What kind of life will you have? It's your CHOICE! And boy, did he emphasize the word "CHOICE!"

CHOICES

"Choices." That word continued to ring in my ears. "What kind of life will you have? It's your CHOICE!" My choice. It's my choice. What kind of life will I have? It's my choice. This was a revelation! This was heavy. Boy, I hadn't used that word in a while! But this was heavy! "It's my CHOICE!" I emphasized that in my thoughts.

That's right! Say it loud and clear. Say it over and over again, so you will never relinquish your authorship to anyone else again. You're writing your life story now. We let so many people co-author our lives! Some people are either telling us what to do and how to do it, or they're taking the credit for it. Then there are those who keep telling us what we should have done. Some telling us what we could have done. Do you hear them? Can you see their faces? I did.

"Sure, there are some people who are there co-authoring our lives at the start, our parents, grandparents, brothers, sisters, other family members and friends too. But they are supposed to be there as guides, as tutors. That's a necessary part of our birth. Remember, 'First the natural, then the spiritual.' People that love us are God's gifts to us to get us started on our lives journey. They are there to bring us, or escort us, really, from the place of our 'natural birth' to the place of our 'spiritual birth.' As long as they are giving us the tools and skills to become the author of our own life, they are fulfilling their part in our 'birth.' Do you see what I mean?"

"Yes, I really do. It's like the Madonna holding the baby Jesus. She was there to bring him into this world and give him the skills and tools he needed to be able to make the choices he would have to in order for him to live the life he planned. The life he planned before he was born. The life he and God, his father, had planned before the world began.

As long as she and others did that, they were a part of his birth process. But when he had been tutored enough, he had to be spiritually born so he could start the process of his metamorphosis!"

"Exactly!" he said, almost shouting it.

"We all have to undergo a metamorphosis. It is paramount in life that we reach a point where we start to fill in the book of our lives with chapters we have written. Not chapters that others have dictated to us."

I had so much to think about. We talked for an hour longer. "CHOICES." It filled my head all the way home. It seemed that God had heard my prayer, or should I say the "cry of my heart?" Because I really hadn't prayed to start this metamorphosis but it was what my heart was crying out for. And I could see how every one of us was supposed to have the same thing happen to us. We were all born into this natural world in order to be born into the spiritual world. What a shame it was, though: so few of us knew that. I guess I was just going to have to do something about that. That was going to be one of the chapters in the book of my life! All the chapters I thought were written in my life's story were not really chapters at all. They were just paragraphs in the first chapter. The chapter called "Birth."

Now I was going to write the chapter after that. I was going to be the author of the book of my life and I was going to do something I'd never really done before. I was going to pray for Divine inspiration and guidance. I had seen that today. There was a God, and I couldn't help but think that He was excited! It was as if God couldn't wait to start to read the book of my life! The book that I was going to author with His help! This was heavy stuff. But it was great stuff! I was so glad that I had met the owner of that bookstore.

Walking home was great. I remembered things that somehow I knew I was supposed to remember. I did forget one thing though. I forgot to ask the owner what his name was! Can you believe it! I didn't even know his name. But I knew something about him. Something I'd read or heard came into my mind as I walked home that day. As the oranges and greens of the leaves and bushes melted into my sight I could hear it clear as a bell, "When the student is ready, the Master will appear." I didn't know him name but I knew he was a "master". Someone who had been writing chapter after chapter in the book of his life for a long time. I wanted to get to know him better. I couldn't wait to tell Barb about him and to go back there again.

She was in the kitchen making dinner when I got home. What a warm feeling I had. I felt so close to her, so secure. She was a part of my birth process. She always had been.

"What's in the bag?" she asked.

"Bookends," I said. "The greatest bookends I've ever seen." I took them out of the bag and she said, "It looks like the mysteries of the universe are wrapped up in those bookends." She didn't know just how right she was, or did she?

APPLICATION

Every one of us is called upon by God to undergo a spiritual transformation. To understand this process through God's eyes we need to prayerfully look at three Scriptures in order to see how the Soul undergoes a "Transformation".

In **2 Corinthians 4:16** Paul tells us that "although our Outward Man perishes, the Inner Man is renewed day by day".

In **1 Corinthians 15:31** Paul again says "I die daily".

Lastly, he relates to us in **Romans 12:2** that we should not be "conformed to the blueprint of living the way the world does but be transformed by the renewing of your minds."

Paul uses the example of a Butterfly referring to the process of metamorphosis. This is the transformation of a earthbound worm into totally different creature; the butterfly. The butterfly is not bound to the earth but soars into the "heavenlies".

To understand how we are "transformed" we can refer to two more Scriptures:

Job 25:6 and **Psalms 22:6** In these verses man is likened to a "worm", an earthbound creature that lives to eat and then dies.

Our "transformation" begins when we receive faith in Jesus are Born Again. As it says in **2 Corinthians 5:17** "If anyone is in Christ they are now a New Creation". Just that one act of faith changes or "Transforms" us. But that is just the beginning! The work is not yet finished.

The newly formed butterfly must go through a "great struggle" to get out of its chrysalis! It is hard work and the butterfly has to expend all of its energy to break out of there. But through patience and perseverance it does break out of its chrysalis.

Yet the work is still not over. No, something more must take place before it can begin to fly! The newly hatched butterfly must hang from its chrysalis and flap its wing continually for hours. When it comes out of the chrysalis they are too wet and weak to fly. The flapping of the wings pumps the blood into them and the movement dries them until they are ready to fly. Without that struggle the wings would never get that butterfly up into the air. If it would somehow let go too soon or stop flapping those wings they would never be strong enough to fly!

Once its wings are dry and strong the butterfly can soar up into the sky! It has won the victory and is now truly transformed.

This is how it is for us. We start as a sinner; just a worm. Then Christ gives us a new life and we are Born Again. But that's just the beginning; we are not finished yet.

We must first go through the struggle to get out of our chrysalis. Once that is accomplished we then hang from it and flap our wings until they are dry enough and strong enough to lift us up into the heavens where we can be seated with Christ Jesus, ruling and reigning with Him in our lives!

What is our chrysalis? It's our old way of thinking. It's what the Bible calls "the carnal mind". Scripture makes it clear that the "carnal mind" is an enemy of God and it's the enemy of the New Christian too. That's why Paul makes it clear that the transformation takes place in our MIND. Christ does a finished work in our spirit. There we are His workmanship. But with the transformation of our minds we have to be "co-laborers with Him". His struggle was to give us the

New Birth! Our struggle is to be transformed by the renewing of our minds.!

The "flapping of our wings" is the "putting on of the mind of Christ"! See **Colossians 2:9 & Philippians 2:5**
It is a struggle for us to think the way Jesus would. We need to ask ourselves all the time: WWJD - What Would Jesus Do?

Most Christians today don't know what He would do because they haven't struggled to renew their Minds! They haven't had their "senses exercised to discern good and evil"! They're still drinking the "milk of the Word" and aren't ready for meat yet! They are just hanging around waiting for Jesus to take care of everything and do everything for them!

Well He already did His part! He died on the cross for us. Now we have to do our part. We have to put on the "mind of Christ" and be transformed! Once we begin to do that we will be able to "go on to perfection" as it says in the Book of **Hebrews 5:12-14 & 6:1**

So "flap your wings" butterfly. Keep putting on the mind of the Lord in every situation and you too can soar each day. Your daily Struggles are a necessary part of your Spiritual Transformation. Without them you can never be who God has planned for you to be but through them you will find that you can live a life of faith and hope in Christ! You can ascend up into the Heavenlies

HE MADE UP HIS MIND

Luke 9:51 "And it came to pass, when the time was come that he should be received up, he steadfastly set his face like flint to go to Jerusalem…"

He knew what lay before Him but He made up His mind that nothing would stop Him from finishing the course set out before Him.

Hebrews 12:11-13 (NASB) "All discipline (*chastening*) for the moment seems not to be joyful, but sorrowful; yet to those who have been trained by it, afterwards it yields the peaceful fruit of righteousness. Therefore, strengthen the hands that are weak and the knees that are feeble, and make straight paths for your feet…."

It took "discipline" for Jesus to go through what He did. He saw that the "chastening" he was going through was going to be horrible but that "afterward" it would yield a glorious reward and "therefore" He "set His face like a flint". He made up His mind and went onward.

Again, the Book of Hebrews tells admonishes us to keep our eyes fixed on Jesus as we "run the race" of life…

Hebrews 12:1 - 2 (NLT) Therefore, since we are surrounded by such a huge crowd of witnesses to the life of faith, let us strip off every weight that slows us down, especially the sin that so easily trips us up. And let us run with endurance the race God has set before us. *We do this by keeping our eyes on Jesus*, the champion who initiates and perfects our faith. Because of the joy awaiting him, he endured the cross, disregarding its shame. Now he is seated in the place of honor beside God's throne.

We will find the place of honor too as we go through the "great struggle" to be transformed.

DID YOU HEAR ABOUT PAT?

Ever heard of Pat Cohan? I didn't think so. Let me tell you about her. Pat was involved in a car accident and due to that accident, she had a bad back, shoulder and hip. She had to take one medicine after another in order to make it through the day. One day she looked at herself, saw all the medicines in her medicine cabinet, and realized that she was not getting better at all. She was rather growing worse and worse. Each area of sickness she had wore her body down a little bit more until the result was that she was on a downward spiral into helplessness and pain.

Pat decided that she was no longer going to be held captive by her body and she started to work out at a gym. She started to build all the muscles around her weak areas. She started to bench press weights. She liked that best because it was done lying down on her back. Her bad spine, shoulder and hip didn't keep her from doing it and so she worked at it and eventually she saw some amazing results.

As she was working out one day her trainer came to her and asked her why she didn't go into competitive weight lifting. She thought he was crazy but he showed her that she was only a short way from the record bench press for a woman in her age bracket.

She was taken totally by surprise and with a grin, like that cat that ate the canary; she said she would go for it. The rest is history! Pat Cohan went on to break the record and while doing that she set a National Record for women her class and age.

You see, she was already in a miserable state of affairs. She had nothing to lose and a lot to gain. She got tired of being in the state she was in and **she made up her mind** that she would change it! She **"set her face like a flint"** and went ahead!

Sure there would be "discipline", a "chastening" of her body. But, she saw the "glorious reward" of accomplishment that lay ahead and "therefore" she undertook the task.

By the way, she also has done another amazing feat. She embarked on a journey that most people would never try to start. In her late 50's, she decided to make the climb to the base camp of Mount Everest! That camp is 17,500 feet above sea level. She said that she did it one step and three breaths at a time! One step and three breaths at a time. Imagine that!

What are the areas of weakness in your life? Where is the pain in your body? What are the limits you perceive for yourself? Pat said that if she could do it, anyone could. How about you? She strengthened the areas around her weak parts. She disciplined herself with the correct activity on a daily basis. She made up her mind that life was for living, not for complaining and set her face towards her Jerusalem! Yes there would be resistance. Yes there would be agony of a sort. Nevertheless, the glorious reward that lay ahead far outshined and outweighed the discipline. She knew that the road to glory was taken "one step and three breaths at a time".

ABOUT THE AUTHOR

Frank Duprée was raised in Long Island, NY and in 1979 he and his wife Giovanna came to New Jersey to Pastor Living Water Church in North Arlington. Along with over 30 years of Pastoral experience, he also holds a Doctoral Degree in Biblical Studies. He was a Radio Evangelist in the NY/NJ area in the 1980's hosting The Meadowlands Ministries Radio Broadcast for over 7 years on WWDJ.

He has also been on staff as a visiting Bible Teacher at Pinecrest Bible Training Center, which was founded by the late Dr. Wade E. Taylor; his Spiritual Father.

Frank has been a Guest Speaker in Conventions in the Northeast as well as a speaker in many local Churches in the New York / New Jersey area. He flows in both a Prophetic and Healing Anointing. He has also traveled to Rio de Janeiro where he ministered to over 3,000 people.

Besides his Teaching and Preaching ministry, he is also an accomplished Singer and Worship Leader.

In January 2000 Frank founded Metro Apostolic Network, which is a fellowship of leaders in the New Jersey Metro Area. Metro Apostolic Network brings Ascension Gift Ministers together with Marketplace Ministers helping to fulfill the need there is today for networking and resource facilitation to advance the Kingdom of God and helping to strengthen both Local Churches and the City Church.

Visit my website:
www.FrankDupree.com

On the website you will see my Home Church
Living Water Church
The Church founded by Frank & his wife Giovanna in 1979

Metro Apostolic Network
The Ministerial Fellowship founded in 2000

Frank Duprée Enterprises
The business part of my Ministry

Teaching
Here you will find years of Frank's work

Psalms 32 ver 5-7

1 John v 9   Hebrews 13 v.5-6

Deut. 30 v 19

Ps. 139   Proverbs 26 v.27

Ephesians 2 Ve 10
                5 v 19
2 timothy 1 v 7   John 16 v 13

Isaiah 54 ve 4 Romens 8 v 18
            61 ver 3

Romans 4 24-25
            5-3-5
Isa. 61 v 1
        53 v 5
Mark 11 ver 25